At a Glance Series   DVD and Lesson Book

DVD Electric Blues

Written by Chad Johnson and Kurt Plahna
Video Performers: Wolf Marshall, Doug Boduch, and Tom Kolb

ISBN: 978-1-4234-9489-8

HAL•LEONARD® CORPORATION
7777 W. BLUEMOUND RD. P.O. BOX 13819 MILWAUKEE, WI 53213

Visit Hal Leonard Online at
www.halleonard.com

Table of Contents

INTRODUCTION

Welcome to *DVD Electric Blues*, from Hal Leonard's exciting At a Glance series. Not as in-depth and slow-paced as traditional method books, the material in *DVD Electric Blues* is presented in a snappy and fun manner intended to have your guitar cryin' in virtually no time at all. Plus, the At a Glance series uses real songs by real artists to illustrate how the concepts you're learning are applied in some of the biggest hits of all time. For example, in *DVD Electric Blues*, you'll learn licks from 19 classics, including "The Thrill Is Gone," "Pride and Joy," "Sweet Little Angel," "Sweet Home Chicago," and more.

Additionally, each book in the At a Glance series comes with a DVD containing video lessons that correspond to the printed material. The DVD that accompanies this book contains four video lessons, each approximately 8 to 14 minutes in length, which correspond to each chapter. In these videos, ace instructors will show you in great detail everything from the basic 12-bar blues progression to the most visceral Stevie Ray string bend. As you work through this book, try to play the examples first on your own; then check out the DVD for additional help or to see if you played them correctly. As the saying goes, "A picture is worth a thousand words." So be sure to use this invaluable tool on your quest to learning the blues.

BLUES PROGRESSIONS

The blues is a ubiquitous style of music that has roots going back hundreds of years. Practically every style of today's popular music is saturated with blues-isms: rock, pop, jazz, folk, bluegrass, reggae, you name it—the blues is in there somewhere.

Over time, the blues form, characterized by seventh chord progressions and the shuffle or swing feel, developed into multiple variations. In this lesson, we're going to take a good look at all the common blues progression forms, and we'll have some fun playing through them, too.

12-BAR BLUES

The most basic blues progression is the 12-bar blues. You'll see this used in literally thousands of songs. You could almost say it is the standard working formula for American popular music.

First we'll play a 12-bar blues in A using seventh chords: A7, D7, and E7. You'll also hear this referred to as the I, IV, and V chords in the key of A.

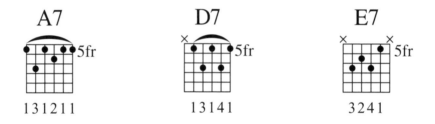

 Ok, here's our first 12-bar blues. Remember to use a shuffle feel, so that the eighth notes sound like the first and last notes of a triplet. Watch the DVD to hear how this sounds.

Sound familiar? It should!

Quick Change

Let's try a variation on this form by adding what is known as a "quick change" in measure 2. With the quick change, instead of staying on the I chord for the first four bars, you switch to the IV chord for measure 2 and then back to the I chord for measures 3 and 4. In the key of A, it would look like this.

The quick change is at least as common as the standard form, if not more so.

Turnaround

Another common variation we can add to the 12-bar is called a *turnaround*. With a turnaround, we're adding a quicker I–IV–I–V change in the last two bars of the progression. This effectively "turns you around" back to the I chord in measure 1.

Let's play another 12-bar in A with both the quick change and the turnaround.

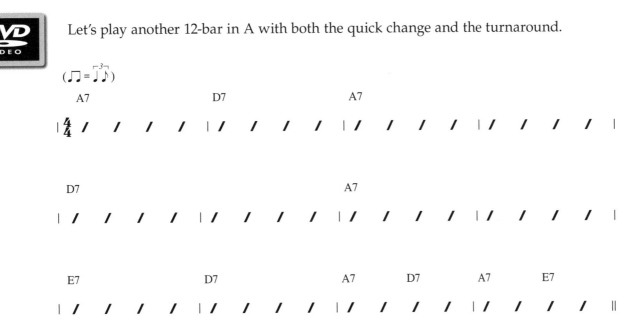

And now let's hear the 12-bar form in action with Robert Johnson's classic, "Sweet Home Chicago." Instead of strumming full chords, we're navigating the changes here with a boogie-woogie bass-style riff for each chord.

"SWEET HOME CHICAGO"
Robert Johnson

Words and Music by
Robert Johnson

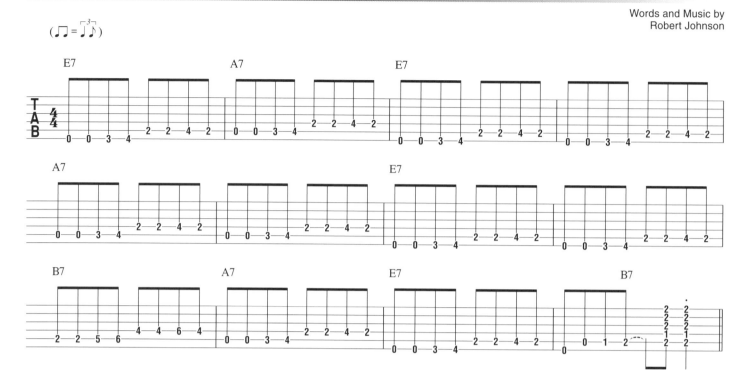

Intros

Sometimes short introductions are added to the 12-bar form. There are several variations used, and we'll check out a few here. This first one is four bars long and starts "from the V," leading you to measure 1 of the 12-bar progression.

Here's another that starts from the V, but it leads to a turnaround-type move that sets you up for measure 1 of the tune.

Endings

Similarly, there are planned endings that can add a nice resolution to a blues tune. Many spontaneous jams wind up in a train wreck at the end because the players haven't bothered to determine how they're going to end! Let's check out a few staples.

This common ending begins on measure 9 of the 12-bar form, taking you from I to IV to V. The final I chord happens on the "and" of beat 2 in the last measure. Cut off the chord and rest for beat 3, then hold the I chord on beat 4.

Another common ending involves a stop on beat 1 of measure 10 so the singer or soloist can sing or play the last line of the song unaccompanied, after which the guitar and/or the rest of the band comes back in for the final two measures with a syncopated hit on the last chord. Check it out.

8-BAR BLUES

Beyond the common 12-bar blues, there are some alternate forms such as the 8-bar blues. Let's play this one first in A, as we have been, and then we'll mix it up a little and play it in C. Here it is in A.

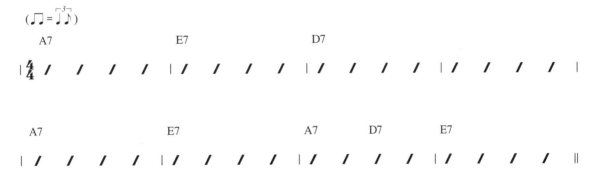

And now let's play it in C. Here are the chords: C7 (I), F7 (IV), and G7 (V)

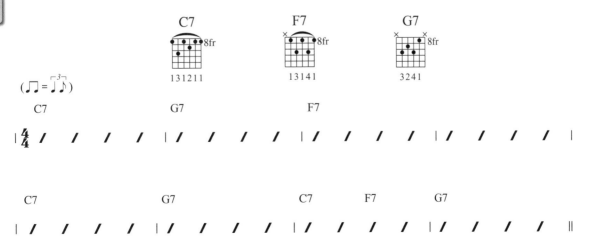

Notice how the V chord comes up more often in the 8-bar blues, giving it a different flavor.

Here's one the most classic 8-bar blues of all time: "Key to the Highway."

"KEY TO THE HIGHWAY"
Big Bill Broozny

Words and Music by Big Bill Broonzy
and Chas. Segar

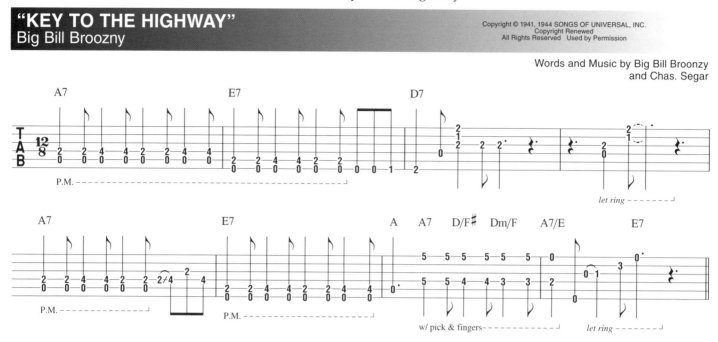

AABA Blues

A variation on the 8-bar form involves the addition of a bridge section, or "B" section, that starts on the IV chord. You play through the usual 8-bar form (or "A" section) twice, then the B section once, and finally back to the A section one more time. This is sometimes referred to as an AABA form.

Let's play it in E this time. Here are the chords: E7 (I), A7 (IV), and B7 (V).

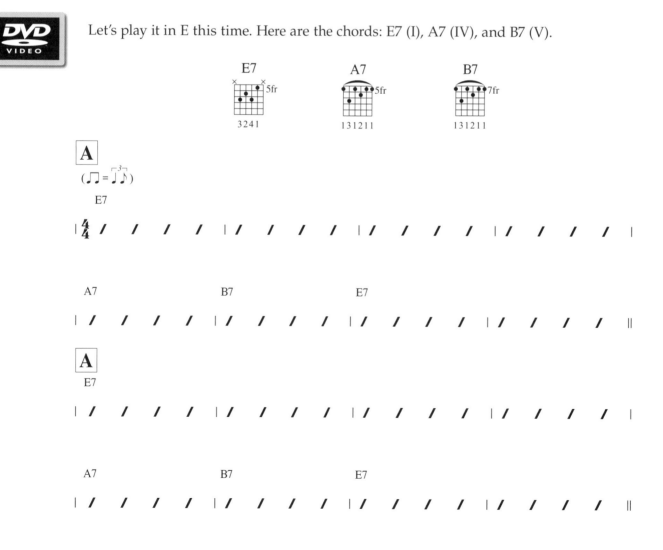

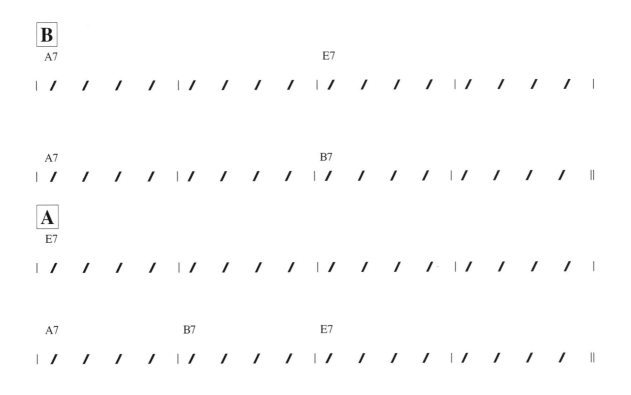

16-BAR BLUES

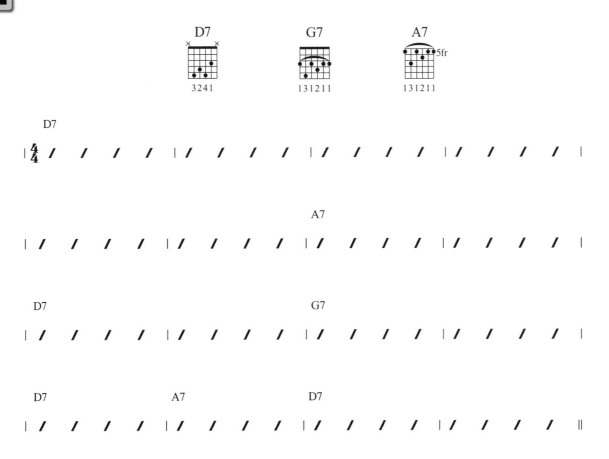

Now let's check out the 16-bar blues. This one often has more of a country or gospel feel, but it can sound straight up blues as well. Let's play it in D. First, the chords: D7 (I), G7 (IV), and A7 (V).

MINOR BLUES

Another interesting variation is the minor blues. Here we use the 12-bar form again, but we replace the I and IV chords with minor chords. Minor blues are often played at a slower tempo as well. Let's play this one in A minor. Here are the chords: Am (i), Dm (iv), and E7 (V).

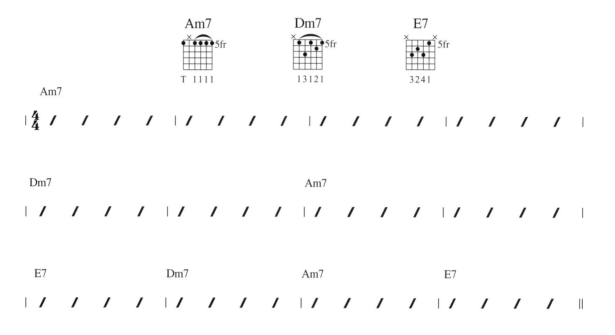

The ♭VI Variation

You can also play a minor blues with a ♭VI chord in measure 9 followed by the V in measure 10. You'll hear this in tunes like "The Thrill Is Gone." We'll play it now in A minor. You'll hear lots of blues played like this—without a shuffle feel—as well.

Watch for the ♭VI chord, Fmaj7, in measure 9. Here's the chord:

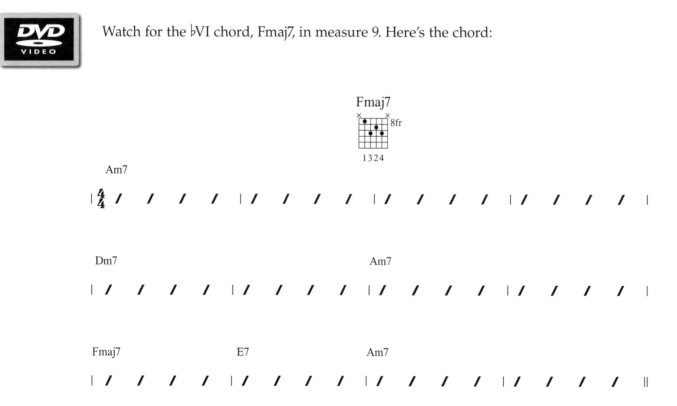

Perhaps the quintessential minor blues is B.B. King's "The Thrill Is Gone." This one is in B minor and uses the ♭VI chord as well. Here's the King of the Blues soloing through the form to open this classic.

"THE THRILL IS GONE"
B.B. King

Words and Music by Roy Hawkins
and Rick Darnell

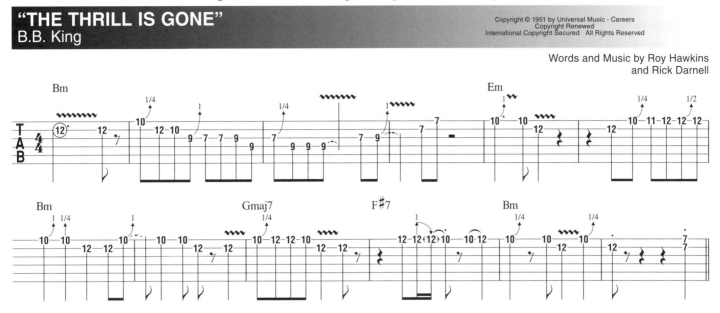

EXTENDED I CHORD

A blues with an extended I chord is somewhat common as well. You play eight measures on the I chord instead of the usual four. After that, the form continues like a regular 12-bar blues. You'll hear this in a blues rhumba, which is heard in classic New Orleans-style blues.

Let's play it in D with a straight feel like the rhumba.

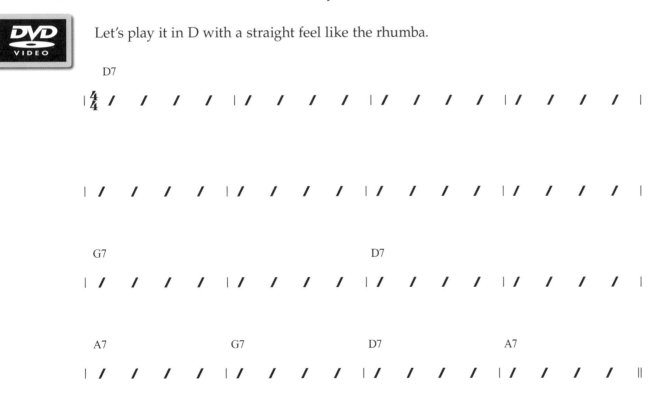

You may have noticed that this example was 16 bars long, yet the form was different than the 16-bar form we played earlier. As you can see, there are many different ways to play a blues.

Here's Willie Dixon's take on this form with "I'm Your Hoochie Coochie Man." Notice how remaining on the I chord for eight measures really builds a lot of tension that's resolved with the arrival of the IV chord in measure 9. He riffs through the entire form, expanding the early minor pentatonic sound into dominant 7th arpeggios at the move to the IV chord.

"I'M YOUR HOOCHIE COOCHIE MAN"
Willie Dixon

Written by Willie Dixon

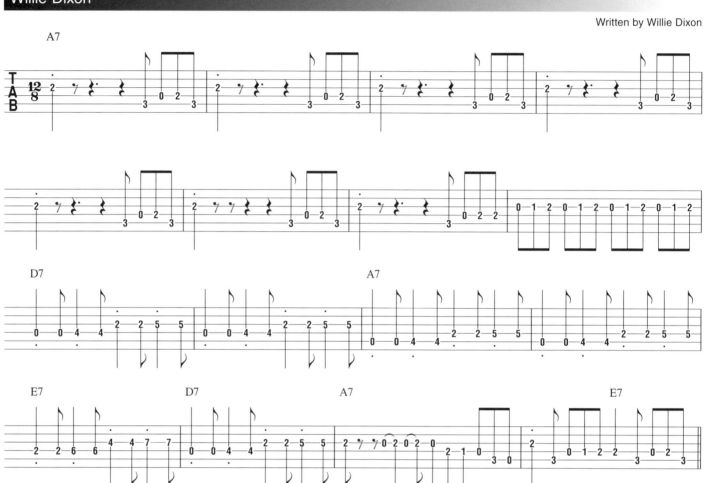

Be sure to try out these progressions in all 12 keys, and soon you'll know them like the back of your fretting hand.

B.B. KING STYLE

B.B. King is perhaps the most celebrated blues guitarist of all time. His contributions to the genre over the last *sixty* years are far-reaching to say the least. Countless guitarists, including Otis Rush, Eric Clapton, Jimi Hendrix, Carlos Santana, Mark Knopfler, Stevie Ray Vaughan, and John Mayer cite B.B. as a huge influence, and his music has undoubtedly shaped the course of blues history.

B.B. developed a very soulful and distinctive single-note style that incorporated his sophisticated string bending and finger vibrato techniques along with a vocal-like fluidity and tone. In this lesson, we're going to study the main elements of the B.B. King style and learn what made him the true King of the Blues.

Blues Boxes

B.B. often favors two scale positions for his lead work: the familiar "box 1" position, and the "B.B. box" position. How many guitarists can say they have a scale named after them?

 B.B. likes to add several notes to this scale, so it's really more of a blues hybrid scale than a pentatonic scale. He adds the major 3rd, 6th, and 9th to the pentatonic box and favors the upper three strings. Note that the lower strings in this box contain only the pentatonic notes as he rarely uses the additional notes in the lower octave. Here's box 1 in the key of A.

 And here's the B.B. box, also in A, which he plays almost exclusively on the top three strings. Notice how he's replaced the ♭7th tone, G, with the sweet-sounding 6th, F♯.

 Here are a couple of licks in the box 1 position in A that B.B. might play. We'll stay in the key of A for this lesson to keep things consistent, but you should also learn everything in different keys as well. This first one works as an intro lick.

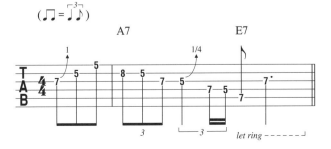

And here's one that uses the 6th and 9th.

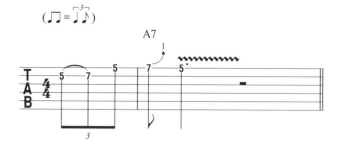

Check out B.B. in action with this lick from "You Upset Me Baby." We're in G here, but this lick starts on the IV chord (C7) and works its way back to the I (G7). Notice how he nicks the added 9th (A) of the G blues hybrid scale, which functions as a 6th over the C7 chord, with a quick hammer-pull move in the second measure and skillfully bends the ♭3rd (B♭) up a half step to the major 3rd (B) over the tonic G7 chord at the end.

"YOU UPSET ME BABY"
B.B. King

Words and Music by B.B. King
and Jules Bihari

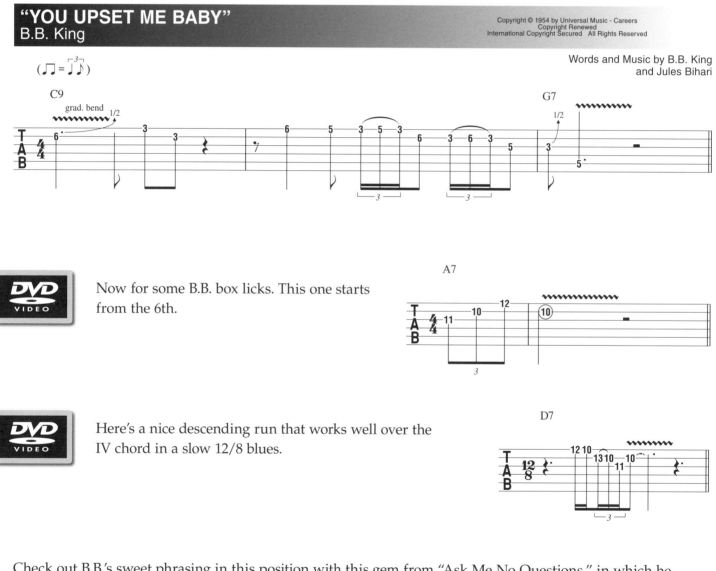

Now for some B.B. box licks. This one starts from the 6th.

Here's a nice descending run that works well over the IV chord in a slow 12/8 blues.

Check out B.B.'s sweet phrasing in this position with this gem from "Ask Me No Questions," in which he mixes staccato and legato notes over the somewhat-rare II–V–I (B7–E7–A7) changes at the end of the form.

"ASK ME NO QUESTIONS"
B.B. King

Words and Music by
B.B. King

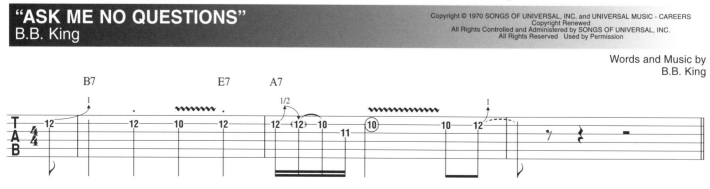

B.B. will also jump between boxes quite fluidly with licks such as this. Take note of the chromatic move on one string in this lick—another B.B.-ism, and a great way to connect boxes within a phrase.

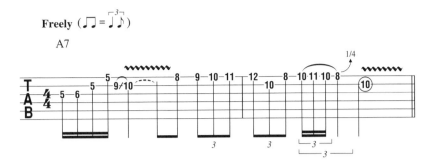

Vibrato

Maybe the most recognizable trait of B.B.'s playing is his signature "hummingbird" vibrato. It's a rapid, singing vibrato that can really make a note come to life. Check out the DVD for a look at the mechanics behind this.

Let's check it out in context with this little lick.

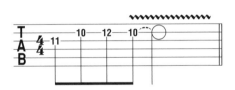

Check out how B.B. decorates the slow blues phrases of "Sweet Little Angel" with his signature vibrato, both on bent and unbent notes.

"SWEET LITTLE ANGEL"
B.B. King

Words and Music by B.B. King
and Jules Bihari

When you're doing vibrato with any of the other fingers, it helps to wrap your thumb around the neck for a little support. Now go back and apply this vibrato technique to some of the licks we learned earlier.

Bending

Another huge part of B.B.'s style is his amazing bending technique and the control that he has over his bends. He constantly bends notes to varying degrees—sometimes quick, subtle quarter-step bends, and other times screaming, sustained bends that cry up a step-and-a-half. Often he'll add vibrato to bent notes.

B.B. has certain signature bend notes that he likes to target, so let's take a look at some of them. We'll play a box 1 position lick with some whole-step bends. On the bends, you should support the bending finger with the other fretting fingers behind it. Maintain pressure on the string as you bend the string upward, toward the ceiling.

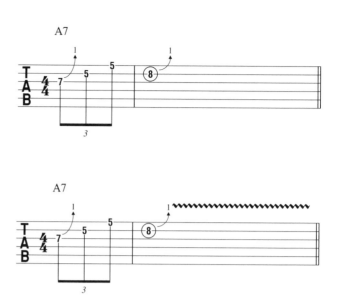

 Now let's play the same lick, but we'll add vibrato to the second bend. Bend to the target pitch first, then, to execute the vibrato, bend it further just a little sharp, and then back down again to the bent pitch, back and forth.

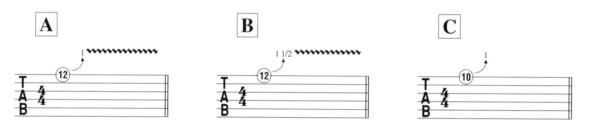

 Let's check out some of his other favorite bends in the B.B. Box in A.

A From the 12th fret up a whole step with some vibrato

B The same note but up a step and a half

C B.B. can also really crank with his index finger. Check out the whole-step bend on the 4th (D) with the index

A **B** **C**

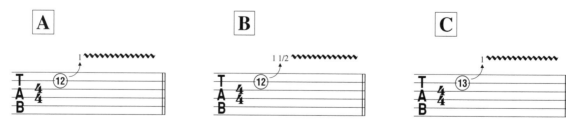

 Here's a series of bends you can do on the second string of the B.B. box.

A **B** **C**

 And let's not forget the quarter-step bend, which works well on pretty much any of these notes. You'll hear B.B. hit the area between the ♭3rd and major 3rd, known as the "true blue note," all the time. This bend is usually done quickly in passing and not as a sustained bend. Here's a lick to demonstrate.

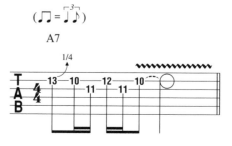

B.B. will often bend several notes in succession to create a speech-like fluidity. Let's check out a B.B. phrase in a slow 12/8 with lots of bending.

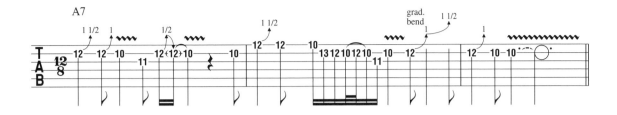

Let's check out some classic B.B. bending licks. Notice how fluidly he combines both half- and whole-step bends.

"JUST LIKE A WOMAN"
B.B. King

By B.B. King

"EVERYDAY I HAVE THE BLUES"
B.B. King

Words and Music by
Peter Chatman

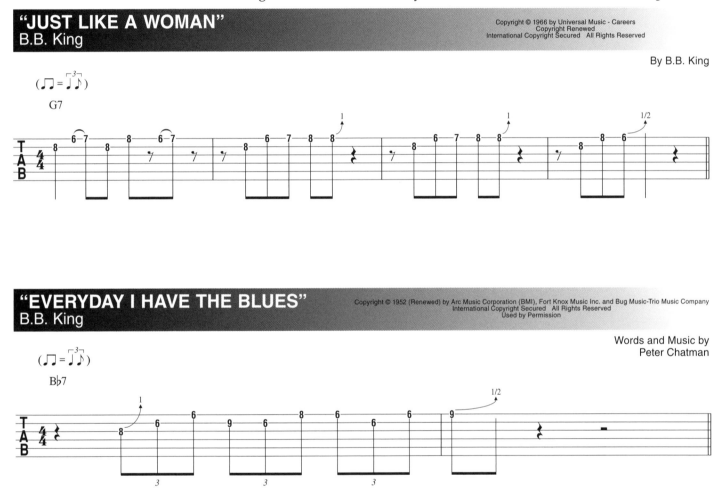

Octaves and Unisons

Mr. King also has some interesting octave and unison tricks up his sleeve. The first one we'll talk about is the octave "yelp." He'll sometimes hit the high tonic note up above the twelfth fret on the first string as a sort of brief punctuation, often as a response to a vocal phrase. He'll mute all the other strings with his first three fingers and fret the note with his pinky. So if we're in A, this would be the seventeenth fret on the first string. Rake the muted strings as you aim for the high note, and slide down afterward.

In "The Thrill Is Gone," he pecks out this yelp repeatedly with sharp staccato articulation on the high octave B note to really make a statement.

"THE THRILL IS GONE"
B.B. King

Words and Music by Roy Hawkins
and Rick Darnell

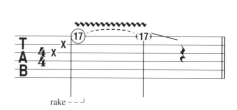

Sometimes he'll hold the note for longer and give it some of his signature vibrato, letting it sing for a while.

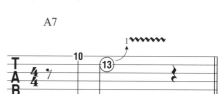

A similar though subtle idea that B.B. throws in here and there involves unison notes. He'll play a note on one string and then quickly bend or slide to a unison note on a lower string.

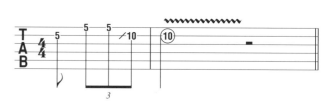

And here's another example of this technique. The unison note is bent to here.

Of course, the best teacher of this style is B.B. himself. Listen to his recordings and pay attention to the small details; his uncanny control and subtle inflections are the essence of his playing.

STEVIE RAY VAUGHAN STYLE

Stevie Ray Vaughan stands as one of the all-time giants of blues guitar and was largely responsible for the huge blues revival in the eighties that's continued to this day. In this lesson, we'll take a look at the major components of Stevie Ray's style.

RHYTHM PARTS

Eric Clapton once remarked that Stevie had more natural talent than anyone he'd ever seen, and this is certainly evident in Stevie's rhythmic feel. His rhythm guitar was often the engine that drove many of his tunes. Let's examine some of his favorite rhythm techniques.

Boogie Woogie Patterns

Stevie played many standard blues rhythm patterns, but he often updated them with a heavy dose of attitude to make them his own. Take this standard boogie bass line figure, for example.

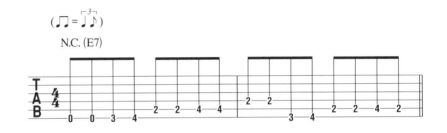

Stevie would use his left hand to mute everything except the string he wanted to sound. This way, he could strum all six strings at once to give every note a lot of weight. Check out the DVD to get a closer look at this technique. The left-hand muting is the key to getting the big sound.

And now let's check out how Stevie did it with the intro riff to "Pride and Joy." Notice that he's getting an even bigger sound by briefly allowing the top three strings to sound on the off-beat upstrokes.

"PRIDE AND JOY"
Stevie Ray Vaughan

Written by Stevie Ray Vaughan

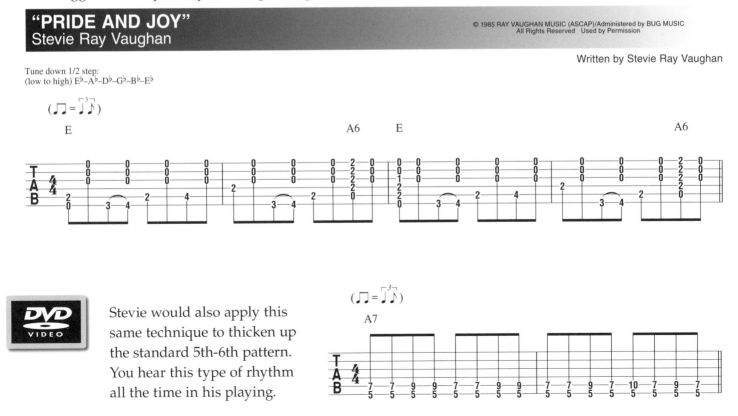

Stevie would also apply this same technique to thicken up the standard 5th-6th pattern. You hear this type of rhythm all the time in his playing.

You can mute with the underside of your first finger and strum through all the strings to get a thicker sound. Check it out on the DVD.

Funky Parts

Stevie also had a funkier side at times. He'd use some 9th voicings and strum them in steady 16th notes, only fully pressing the fret-hand down at strategic points to create syncopated rhythms with percussive clicks in between.

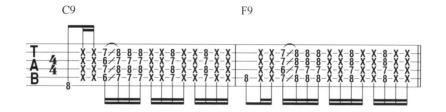

Here's how Stevie used this technique in the verses of "Tightrope." In this part, he omits the percussive dead notes altogether and just pecks out the partial 9th chord voicing stabs in a funky syncopated rhythm.

"TIGHTROPE"
Steveie Ray Vaughan

Written by Stevie Ray Vaughan
and Doyle Bramhall

Tune down 1/2 step:
(low to high) E♭–A♭–D♭–G♭–B♭–E♭

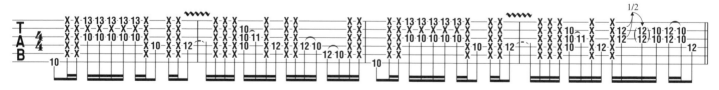

He also had busier funky riffs that mixed chordal playing with single notes. A lot of times, he'd work out of the basic sixth-string barre chord shape but mix notes from minor and major pentatonic scales. The following riff is an example of that style. Notice that the left hand is continuing its muting job so the right hand can strum away freely, and you don't worry about other notes coming out.

We're working out of this basic D barre chord shape here at the tenth fret, using our thumb for the 6th string—the way Hendrix would do it.

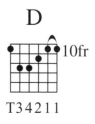

D
10fr

T34211

Check out this ultra-cool riff from "Couldn't Stand the Weather" for a prime example of this approach. Here, Stevie really milks out every possible note from the D barre chord shape.

"COULDN'T STAND THE WEATHER"
Stevie Ray Vaughan

Tune down 1/2 step:
(low to high) E♭–A♭–D♭–G♭–B♭–E♭

Written by Stevie Ray Vaughan

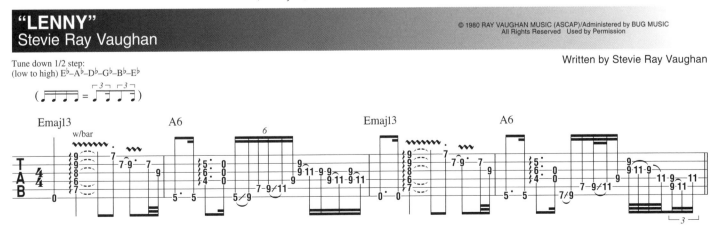

Extended Chords

Stevie also had quite a nice chord vocabulary for a blues guy. This was especially noticeable in his ballads, where he'd often use 6th chords, major 7th chords, and altered dominants. He'd mix a few Hendrixy hammer-on embellishments and whammy bar vibrato to get things like the following example.

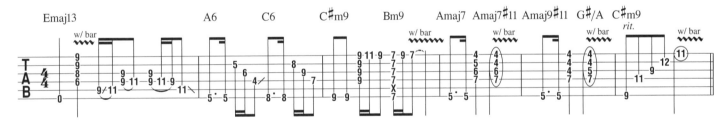

Stevie's beautiful rhythm playing is on full display in "Lenny." Check out the liquid-smooth double stops he uses to lead back into the lush I chord (Emaj13) each time.

"LENNY"
Stevie Ray Vaughan

Tune down 1/2 step:
(low to high) E♭–A♭–D♭–G♭–B♭–E♭

Written by Stevie Ray Vaughan

LEAD PLAYING

Stevie was one of the most exciting, visceral, and impressive lead players in all the blues genre. He had as much chops, taste, and tone as anyone, and he put his entire body into just about every note he played.

Minor Pentatonic Box

For most of his lead playing, he worked out of the standard pentatonic box. In case you're not familiar with it, here it is in A:

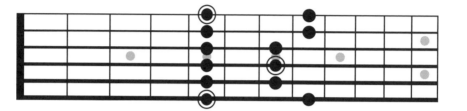

As you probably know, this is a moveable shape that can be played anywhere on the neck in different keys. Let's take a look at some of his favorite licks from this shape. Here's a classic triplet phrase he might play over a shuffle.

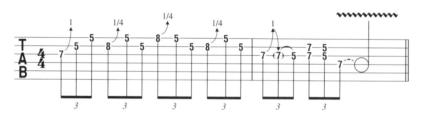

Here's a classic box lick from "Cold Shot."

"COLD SHOT"
Stevie Ray Vaughan

Tune down 1/2 step:
(low to high) Eb–Ab–Db–Gb–Bb–Eb

Words and Music by Mike Kindred
and Wesley Clark

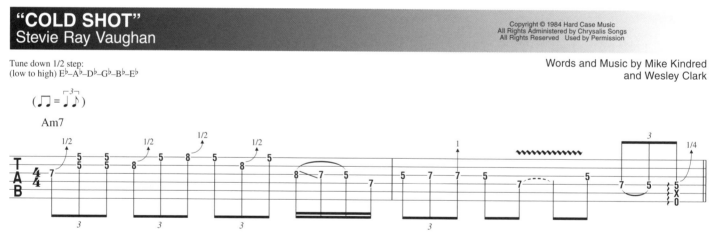

Stevie was a string-bending fool, and this next lick is a good example. It's something he might play over a funkier groove. This one's out of D minor pentatonic box in tenth position.

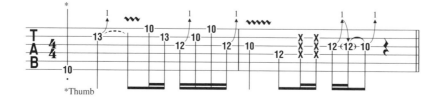

Extended Box Position

Though Stevie stayed in the standard blues box a lot, he knew the blues scale all over the neck. He would also spend a good amount of time in what's known as the "extended box." Here's what it would look like in A:

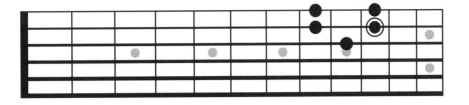

And here are a few typical Stevie phrases in that position. This first one's in A, over a medium shuffle groove.

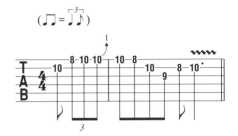

Here's one in E that really sings. Notice the use of upstrokes for the bends and the *first-finger* bend on the fifteenth fret. These details are part of the sound, so don't neglect them.

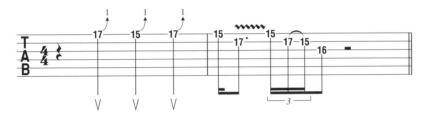

Stevie would also connect these two positions seamlessly into one lick. You get things like the following example in B. Notice that a slide is used to move between the two positions.

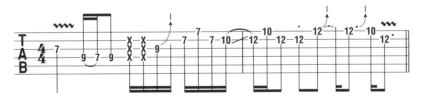

Mixing Minor and Major Pentatonic

A lot of times Stevie would mix the major and minor pentatonics of the same root together to get a brighter sound. In case you don't know it, here's the major pentatonic in A:

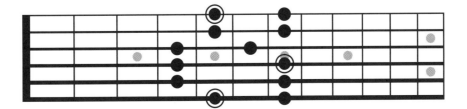

So Stevie would draw from both major and minor in one lick. For example, he may do something like this in E.

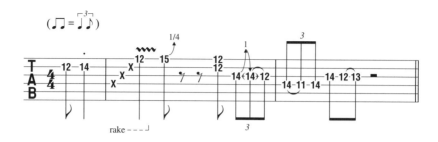

The pick-up notes come from E major pentatonic, but the second measure switches to E minor pentatonic. The last measure then mixes both major and minor pentatonic.

Check out the major-minor mastery Stevie demonstrates in "Lenny." Combining these sounds like he does adds much more depth and complexity to the lines.

"LENNY"
Stevie Ray Vaughan

Tune down 1/2 step:
(low to high) E♭–A♭–D♭–G♭–B♭–E♭

Written by Stevie Ray Vaughan

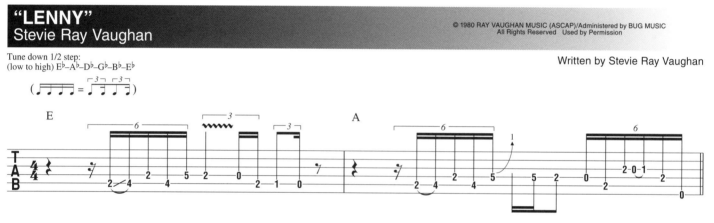

Open-String Licks

Stevie was also a monster when it came to open-position licks. These were almost always in the key of E. Let's take a look at a couple.

This first one would be played over a shuffle groove and is a great example of a classic turnaround lick.

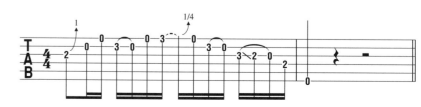

He could also really burn it up down there too, with things like this.

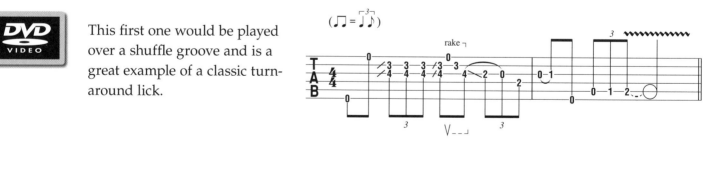

Here's Stevie on an open-position rampage in "Scuttle Buttin'." This one will take some work to get up to tempo for sure!

"SCUTTLE BUTTIN'"
Stevie Ray Vaughan

Tune down 1/2 step:
(low to high) Eb–Ab–Db–Gb–Bb–Eb

Written by Stevie Ray Vaughan

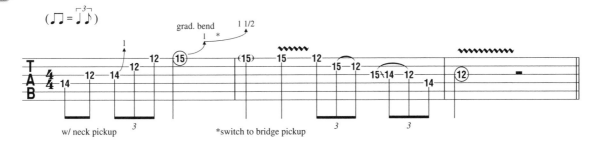

SPECIAL TRICKS

We'll finish off this lesson looking at a few special tricks Stevie used occasionally to keep things interesting.

Changing Pickups

One thing he would do is switch pickups while holding a bend. Starting off on the neck pickup, he'd switch to the bridge pickup during a long bend to really make it come alive.

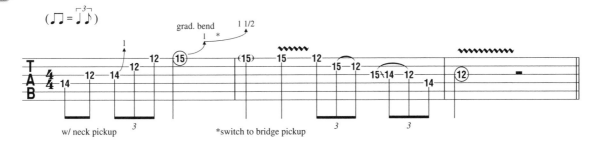

Octave Drop

He'd also abruptly drop down an octave in the middle of a lick to get a dramatic effect. Here's an example in G that starts in the fifteenth position and drops down an octave to the third position. It's a real attention-grabber.

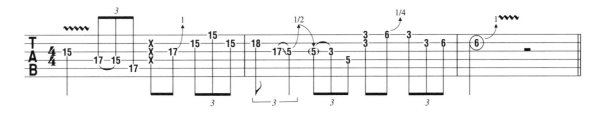

Have fun with these licks and remember to play 'em with conviction!

PROGRESSIVE BLUES LICKS

Have you ever wondered what makes the blues of players like Robben Ford, Larry Carlton, or Scott Henderson sound so progressive or sophisticated? Well, it's not their gear (although in Robben and Larry's case, Dumble amps are sure nice). It's mostly their application of certain musical concepts that are largely drawn from the jazz language. In this lesson, we're going to take a look at those concepts and learn how to infuse your blues lines with that same sophistication.

THE 6TH AND THE 9TH

Most blues players are pretty well versed in the minor pentatonic and the blues scale. Well, we can take a lot of those licks and give them a fresh sound by simply replacing a note here and there. Specifically, the 6th and the 9th are great tones to use. Neither of these tones appear in the minor pentatonic or blues scale. Let's look at how this is done. We'll work in C for this lesson, but you can, and should, transpose these ideas to all keys.

 If we take the minor pentatonic shape and replace the ♭7th, B♭, with the 6th, A, we'll get this:

 Just by doing that, you can get a bit more sophisticated sound. Here's an example.

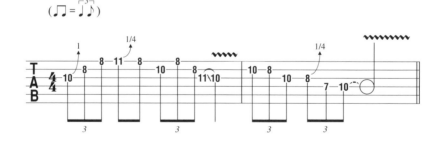

You'll notice that you'll have to abandon the typical box fingering at times with this approach, but with some practice you won't think twice about it.

 A lot of people know the minor pentatonic scale in more than one position, and it's good to do the same with this scale. For example, here's another fingering for the scale based around the fifteenth position mostly.

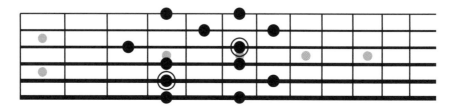

And here's a lick from that form—something Robben Ford might play. The phrasing in this one is a bit more angular, which adds to the sophistication a bit. The fingering can be a little tricky, so follow the suggestions in the music.

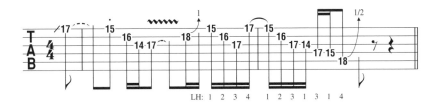

The 9th can be added to the minor pentatonic or blues scale, or it can be used in conjunction with the 6th. You can get things like this.

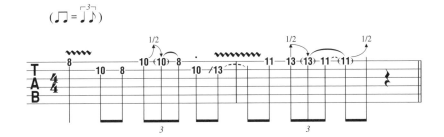

Here's Eric Clapton milking this scale in "I'm Tore Down." Although Slowhand is phrasing here over the V chord (G7), he's working from the C minor pentatonic, nicking both the 9th and the 6th.

"I'M TORE DOWN"
Eric Clapton

Words and Music by
Sonny Thompson

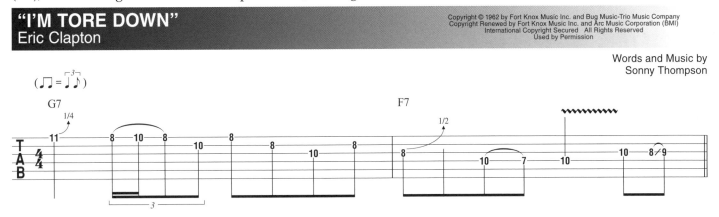

The B.B. King influence is apparent obviously when you play out of the "B.B. box." Try this one. We're using the ♭7th, 6th, ♭3rd, 9th, and even bending to the major 3rd at the end.

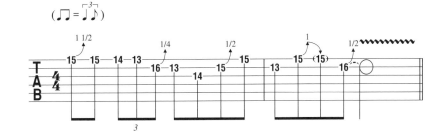

Speaking of the B.B. influence, check out how Robben Ford channels his inner B.B. with this gem from "Talk to Your Daughter," in which he bridges B.B. box licks at the beginning with sassy, bluesy phrasing from the standard box to wrap it up.

"TALK TO YOUR DAUGHTER"
Robben Ford

Words and Music by
John Lee Hooker

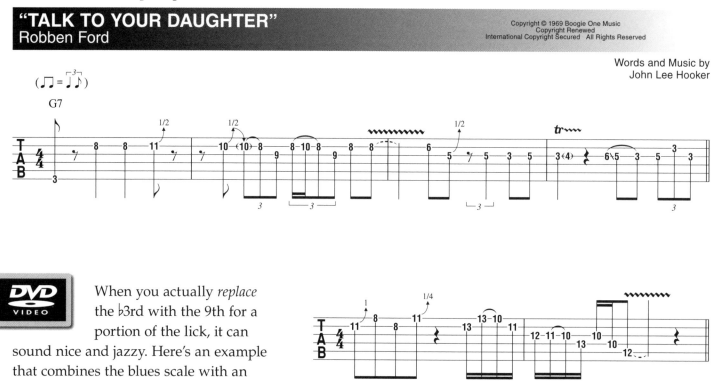

When you actually *replace* the ♭3rd with the 9th for a portion of the lick, it can sound nice and jazzy. Here's an example that combines the blues scale with an added 6th and 9th.

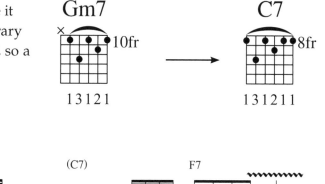

All these things we've talked about so far are things you can do to spice up your blues lines in general when playing over a basic bluesy groove. Now let's talk about specific strategies relating to the 12-bar form.

NAVIGATING THE I–IV MOVE

There are several key points at which you're likely to hear these guys jazz it up a bit. One of the most common spots is the transition from measure 4 to 5, or the I chord to the IV chord, in a 12-bar. In our case, that would be C7 moving to F7.

Superimposing a ii–V Leading to IV

There are lots of things we can do here to make it interesting. The first is superimposing a temporary ii–V leading to IV. In our case, the IV chord is F, so a ii–V leading to that would be Gm7 to C7.

For measure 4, instead of just thinking C7, we could think Gm7 for beats 1 and 2 and C7 for beats 3 and 4. By doing this, something as simple as running up and down arpeggios could sound fairly hip.

By the way, playing sixteenth notes over a shuffle groove like this is known as *double timing*. You'll hear guys like Robben Ford do it a lot.

Now if you've studied jazz at all, and these guys have certainly done that, you'll know that there are plenty of ways to play over ii–Vs. And pretty much all of those ways are valid here.

 One way to hip things up is to alter the V chord in our superimposed ii–V progression. In this case, we're talking about altering the C7 that leads to F. So, instead of thinking of this chord:

C7
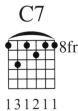
1 3 1 2 1 1

 We'll be thinking about maybe a C7#5:

C7#5
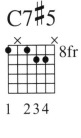
1 2 3 4

 Or maybe a C7b5:

C7b5
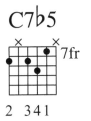
2 3 4 1

 When the V chord is altered like this, it really wants to resolve even more so than normal. A great choice for playing over a dominant chord with an altered 5th is the **whole tone scale**. In our case, since the altered chord is a C7, we'd use the C whole tone scale. Here's a fingering for that in seventh and eighth position.

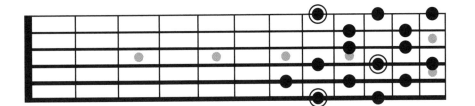

 Because it's nothing but whole steps, it's only a six-note scale. Now let's incorporate it into a lick.

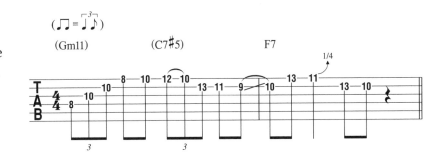

 This lick begins with a Gm11 arpeggio, from this chord shape:

Gm11
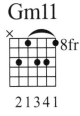
2 1 3 4 1

Then we move into C whole tone and resolve to the 3rd of F7, which is A.

Here's another example where we're playing a straight C blues scale for the first part of the measure and then move into C whole tone for the second half. In this instance, we're kind of ignoring the ii chord in our superimposed ii–V and just concentrating on the altered V. This type of approach is also a possibility—one you might hear Scott Henderson do.

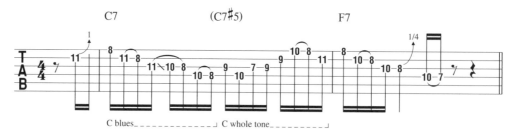

You can also imply a *fully* altered chord, which would have an altered 9th as well. Then you might have these types of C7 chords:

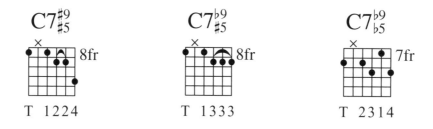

The scale of choice for this situation actually has several names, but we'll call it the **altered scale**. Here's a fingering in C:

Now let's hear the C altered scale in action.

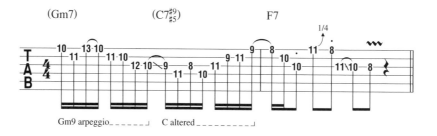

The other spot in a standard blues where you have a V to I relationship is at the turnaround, where the actual V of the key, in our case, G7, resolves to C at the top of the form. So it makes sense that you can transpose all these ideas for that chord. Here's an example of that, in a straight eighths feel, starting at measure 11 on the I chord and moving through the turnaround. We're playing G whole tone over the altered G7 chord. Notice how we take advantage of the symmetrical fingering of the whole tone scale—the same thing two frets down—several times throughout the lick.

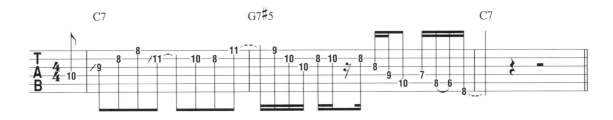

Robben Ford whips out this ear-grabbing altered scale lick in "Help the Poor." The home key is D minor, and he's playing the A altered scale here over the V chord (A13sus4–A7#5).

"HELP THE POOR"
Robben Ford

Words and Music by
Charlie Singleton

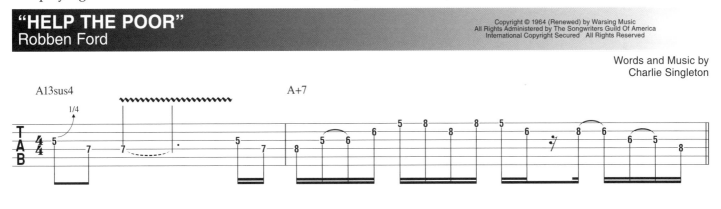

DORIAN MODE IN MINOR KEYS

Let's finish up with a few more concepts that you can use in general to spice up your blues lines. When you're playing over a bluesy minor groove, using the Dorian mode can get a great, angular sound. Here's an example in a straight-8ths mid-tempo groove—maybe like "The Thrill Is Gone" or "Help the Poor." We start and end pentatonic, but slip a Dorian line in the middle.

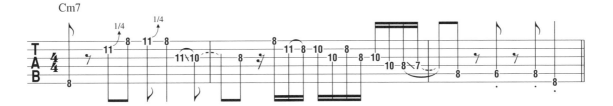

Here's fusion master Scott Henderson peppering a C minor blues, "Tore Down House," with a bit of the C Dorian flavor.

"TORE DOWN HOUSE"
Scott Henderson

Written by Scott Henderson

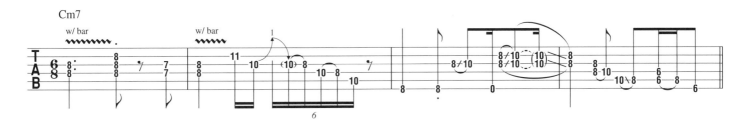

CHROMATICS OR SIDE-SLIPPING

Another great concept to use, in major or minor blues, is the use of *chromatics* or *side-slipping*. You can take a fragment, say two notes, and move it by half steps for just a bit before locking back in to the home key. This works especially well in a double-time line. Here's an example over the same type of straight-eighths minor groove. After a few C minor pentatonic phrases, we run up a Cm7 arpeggio in the next position and then slip through Bm pentatonic and B♭m pentonic (just two notes each) before landing back on C.

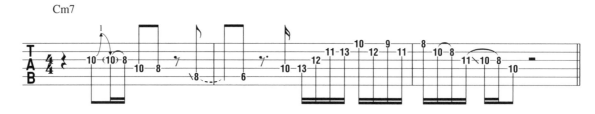

And here's another example over a major blues with a shuffle groove. Notice that we're taking an 9th arpeggio fragment (E–D–B♭–G) and moving it up chromatically twice before ending with a whole tone-sounding F♯–C, which leads perfectly to F.

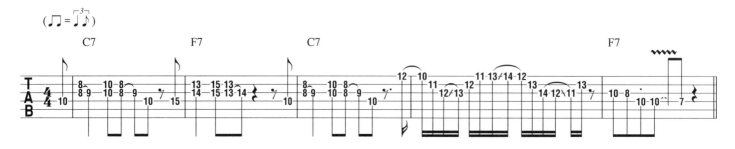

Hopefully, you've enjoyed our journey and learned some new approaches to try out on your blues licks. There's a lot of information here, so work through it slowly. And don't forget to listen to your favorite players to hear these ideas in action!